THE SECRET OF SUCCESS: UNLEASHING YOUR POTENTIALS.

BARNETT   *BUCKLEY*

FIRST EDITION

TABLE OF CONTENT

INTRODUCTION

Success is a notion that has diverse connotations for many people. Achieving personal objectives, finding fulfillment in one's work, making a substantial contribution to society, or just leading a meaningful life are all examples of what might be meant by this. The capacity to realize one's potential is a trait shared by people who excel in their respective industries, despite the fact that different people's definitions of success may differ.

The act of using one's intrinsic talents, abilities, and skills to accomplish desired results is known as "unleashing potentials." It entails identifying one's skills, building on them, establishing a growth mindset, and making proactive moves toward one's own and one's career's progress.

It is crucial to adopt a holistic perspective that takes into account several facets of our lives, such as our attitude habits objectives relationships and self-awareness, in order to properly grasp success and unlock our potentials. It necessitates a thorough awareness of our passions, special talents, and flaws.

Success is a journey that calls for perseverance, resilience, and adaptation rather than a destination. It entails establishing specific objectives, coming up with a strategy, and being prepared to push ourselves outside our comfort zones. It also calls for constant learning, taking chances, and viewing failure as an opportunity for improvement.

Success is also not restricted to a single aspect of life. It encompasses our interpersonal connections, physical and mental health, career objectives, and general sense of contentment. When we reach our full potential, we may create harmony and balance in all aspect of our lives and feel intense happiness and fulfillment.

Moreover, realizing the significance of mentality is necessary for understanding success and realizing our potential. Our thoughts and beliefs have a big impact on how we act and how things turn out. By adopting a growth mindset, we may build resilience, conquer challenges, and have a good attitude even when faced with setbacks.

Success also frequently depends on our capacity to capitalize on our advantages.

Chapter 1

SELF-AWARENESS:

UNCOVERING AND LEVERAGING YOUR STRENGTH

Self-awareness is essential for fostering personal development. It entails being aware of and comprehending your own feelings, ideas, and strengths and flaws. Finding and using your strengths is a crucial component of self-awareness that may significantly influence your path to success and joy.

It takes a great deal of introspection and self-reflection to identify your talents. You must be honest with yourself while answering tough questions. What are your areas of strength? What facets of your personality are admired by others? What gives you contentment and joy? Examining your former victories and "flow" moments may also provide you a lot of insight into your skills.

Getting other people's opinions is another smart move. Speak to your close friends, family, coworkers, and mentors. They may provide you a fresh perspective on your advantages that you hadn't thought of. Your self-awareness may be strengthened and validated by their observations.

It's crucial to accept and work with your limitations in addition to your talents. Knowing your limitations frees you up to concentrate on developing yourself. It assists you in identifying areas where you must put in work and investment to reach your full potential.

Leveraging your abilities entails making the most of them in many areas of your life. For instance, if you have excellent communication skills, you may use them in leadership positions or in your professional connections with others. You may increase your chances of success and fulfillment by matching your talents with your objectives.

Seeking for chances to use your abilities is one approach to make the most of them. Look for work, positions, or initiatives that fit your inherent skills. When you are in a situation where you can utilize your skills, you frequently feel in the zone and satisfied, which encourages further growth and achievement.

Additionally, self-awareness can aid in your understanding of how to interact and work effectively with others. A spirit of collaboration and mutual support is fostered by being aware of your own capabilities as well as the strengths of others around you. It may result in more beneficial and peaceful interpersonal interactions on both a personal and professional level.

But self-awareness shouldn't stop at only recognizing one's advantages. It also entails being aware of your shortcomings and potential growth areas. Adopt a development attitude, which recognizes that with effort and commitment, deficiencies may be turned into strengths. To keep your skill set up to date, look for learning and development opportunities.

Self-awareness is a potent instrument for achievement and personal development. Finding and utilizing your strengths can enable you to better match your interests and skills with your objectives and achieve more pleasure and fulfillment. Accept self-analysis, be open to learning and improvement, and ask for comments. You can achieve your full potential and take big steps in the direction of a fulfilling life if you do this.

1.1 THE POWER OF SELF-AWARENESS

Although self-awareness is a crucial component of success and personal development, it is frequently underrated. The capacity to reflect on and comprehend one's own ideas, feelings, strengths, and flaws is known as self-awareness. It serves as the cornerstone upon which people may make better informed decisions, overcome obstacles, and lead real lives.

We learn important things about our desires, anxieties, and motives when we are self-aware. This information makes it easier for us to recognize and build upon our talents, allowing us to do so successfully. Recognizing our skills enables us to use them in both our personal and professional efforts, whether they be excellent communicators, problem-solvers, or compassionate listeners.

Additionally, self-awareness allows us to examine and take care of our shortcomings. We may actively work on bettering ourselves if we are aware of and tolerant of our limits. This could entail looking for help from others or pursuing more education and skill development. Weaknesses can eventually be turned into strengths and opportunities for development.

The effect that self-awareness has on our interpersonal connections is another potent quality. Understanding our feelings and impulses helps us become more aware of how our actions impact people around us. This knowledge encourages empathy and enables us to handle interpersonal situations with more tact and understanding. We may communicate more efficiently, settle disputes, and create deeper connections by becoming aware of our triggers and habits.

Decision-making also heavily relies on self-awareness. We may make decisions that are in line with our true selves when we are aware of our values and beliefs. This lessens the possibility of making choices inconsistent with our aims and goals. Being self-aware allows us to make decisions that enhance our overall well-being and personal pleasure.

Additionally, self-awareness fosters a positive outlook. Understanding our feelings and ideas helps us control them more skillfully. When dealing with stress-related setbacks and difficulties, we become less reactive and more proactive. We may overcome challenges more easily and confidently by developing resilience and concentrating on solutions rather than problems.

Self-awareness development is a lifetime process. It calls for persistent self-reflection, asking difficult questions, and being receptive to criticism and personal development. Self-awareness may be increased by activities like writing, practicing mindfulness, and getting counseling or coaching.

As a result, self-awareness has the power to help us realize our full potential and live lives that are more meaningful and fulfilling. We may develop lasting relationships, overcome barriers, and make conscious decisions by realizing and appreciating our talents and flaws. A transforming tool, self-awareness enables us to live truthfully and have a beneficial influence on both our own lives and the lives of others.

1.2 IDENTIFYING YOUR STRENGTH AND WEAKNESSES

Self-awareness is essential for controlling our emotions and preserving our mental health. We may perceive and accept our feelings without condemnation or repression when we are self-aware. This enables us to successfully control our emotions and lessens the possibility that we may experience overwhelming unpleasant emotions or impulsive behaviors.

Furthermore, self-awareness improves our capacity to devise and work toward worthwhile objectives. We may better match our aims with our real selves by being aware of our basic beliefs and desires. This alignment gives us a feeling of direction and purpose, which increases our drive and dedication to accomplish what matters most to us.

Self-awareness aids in both individual and collective development. Knowing our strengths and shortcomings allows us to look for areas where we can grow and develop. By utilizing our strengths, we may reach our full potential and look for ways to improve in areas where we may not be as strong. Continual self-improvement boosts one's competence and sense of competence.

Additionally, self-awareness enables us to live more consciously and effectively. By being aware of our cognitive biases and beliefs, we may challenge presumptions and take into account opposing viewpoints. We may make decisions based on our principles and long-term goals rather than being primarily influenced by outside factors or social expectations thanks to critical thinking.

Self-awareness also promotes flexibility and resilience. We can negotiate change and obstacles with better flexibility and emotional stability when we are aware of our strengths and shortcomings. We are more receptive to criticism, eager to learn from our errors, and more prepared to modify our strategy when faced with challenges.

In conclusion, the strength of self-awareness rests in its capacity to change our lives and enable us to live really and intentionally. We may utilize our abilities, fix our deficiencies, establish stronger relationships, make wise decisions, and pursue meaningful objectives by accepting who we actually are. Self-awareness development is a lifetime path that calls for openness, contemplation, and a dedication to personal development. Our potential is unlocked as we increase our self-awareness, and this has a beneficial knock-on impact on both our own lives and the lives of people around us.

1.3 STRATEGIES FOR LEVERAGING YOUR STRENGTH

Self-awareness is advantageous for our interpersonal connections as well as for our personal development. Being self-aware helps us better understand and control our actions, feelings, and reactions, which has a good effect on how we connect with others. In contrast to reacting impulsively, we may deliberately select how we respond by being aware of our triggers, biases, and habits. This encourages better and more effective communication, which strengthens connections and creates relationships with more depth.

Being self-aware also gives us the ability to accept responsibility for our choices and actions. Understanding our beliefs, motives, and priorities allows us to make decisions that are in line with what is most important to us. This sense of ownership enables us to accept responsibilities for both our accomplishments and failings, fostering personal accountability and development.

Additionally, self-awareness helps us to comprehend and empathize with people better. We can relate to and sympathize with others' experiences more effectively when we are conscious of our own emotional struggles and weaknesses. This empathy makes it easier for us to relate to individuals more deeply, which fosters a sense of respect, trust, and support amongst people.

Self-awareness is highly regarded and sought after in professional situations. People with high levels of self-awareness are frequently viewed as great leaders because they are aware of their own talents and shortcomings and know how to use them to their advantage. They also foster a culture of growth and development within their teams by being more receptive to criticism and lifelong learning.

The ability of self-awareness to help us get in touch with our genuine selves is ultimately what gives it its power. It enables us to make decisions that are in line with our beliefs and objectives while living a genuine and intentional life. Self-awareness is the first step on a transformational path that enables us to reach our greatest potential and lives more contentedly and meaningfully.

Chapter 2

GOAL SETTING AND PLANNING:
MAPPING YOUR PATH TO SUCCESS

Success is a deliberate result of setting goals and carefully planning; it does not happen by accident. Your chances of succeeding in any area of your life can be considerably increased by setting clear and doable goals. Understanding the principles of efficient goal setting and planning will help you lay out your route to success, whether you're trying to succeed in your personal life, your career, your schooling, or any other effort.

When it comes to goal-setting and planning, keep in mind the following important tips:

1. *Define Your Vision:* Start by picturing your end goal. How do you define success? Having a clear vision serves as a compass during the goal-setting process and aids in understanding what you genuinely seek.

2. *Establish* SMART *Goals:* SMART goals are time-bound, specific, measurable, achievable, and relevant. Make your goals measurable, realistic, pertinent to your vision, and time-bound when you set them. Structure and concentration are provided by SMART goals, making it simpler to monitor progress and make changes as needed.

3. *Break it Down:* It might be difficult to keep motivated when big goals seem overwhelming. Divide your lofty objectives into smaller, more manageable activities. By doing so, you can celebrate accomplishments along the way and stay motivated. This not only makes them less intimidating.

4. *Develop an Action Plan:* Specify the steps needed to accomplish each goal in a thorough action plan. Determine the proper timelines for each work and the resources, expertise, and support you require. Your goals can be transformed into a practical roadmap with the aid of an organized action plan, which keeps you organized and motivated.

5. Remain Devoted: Setting goals successfully demands dedication and commitment. Particularly when facing challenges and setbacks, persistence is essential. Maintain your vision in mind, keep a good attitude, and change your plans as needed. Keep in mind that failures are occasions for development and education.

6. Regularly Review Your Progress and Make Adjustments: Regularly analyzing your progress enables you to assess your approach and make the required modifications. Examine your progress and see whether any changes are necessary or if any new opportunities have arisen. Successful planning requires a high degree of adaptability and flexibility.

7. Maintain Accountability: Tell a trustworthy friend, family member, or mentor about your objectives so they can help you stay accountable. Regular check-ins and discussions about your progress can be a great source of encouragement and support.

8. Celebrate Milestones: Take time to recognize your progress. Recognizing and rewarding oneself for achieving goals, no matter how modest, is crucial. The motivation is increased, and constructive behavior is reinforced.

9. Remain Concentrated: Limit interruptions and order your objectives. It's simple to feel pushed in several directions, but focusing on your goals will help you stay on track and avoid diluting your efforts.

10. Have Confidence in Yourself: Stay confident and self-assured throughout your path. Remind yourself that success is possible with the appropriate attitude and relentless effort. Have faith in your talents.

Keep in mind that planning and goal-setting are ongoing processes that call for continual examination and revision. You may effectively design your road to success and attain your goals in a meaningful and purposeful way by putting these secrets into practice and incorporating them into your life.

2.1 SETTING **SMART** GOALS

The key to success is to set SMART goals. Specific Measurable Achievable Relevant and Time-bound is the abbreviation for SMART. Your chances of accomplishing your goals and reaching the peak of success increase if you include these five components in them.

First, being explicit when creating goals is crucial. Goals that are too generic or vague are hard to visualize and lack direction. Specify the precise result you want in order to make your goals more explicit. For instance, you can be more precise by expressing "I want to lose 10 pounds and be able to run 5 kilometers in three months" as opposed to just "I want to get in shape." Clear objectives provide you direction and help you concentrate your efforts more successfully.

Secondly, your objectives should also be quantifiable. It's essential to monitor and assess your development as you go. Quantifiable goals, such as percentages of numbers or dates, allow you to evaluate your progress in an objective manner. For instance, if you want to improve your monthly sales, you can set a measurable objective of doing so within the next six months by increasing sales by 10%. Measuring your progress helps you stay accountable while also inspiring you and giving you a sense of accomplishment as you get closer to your objective.

Next, goals should also be feasible. Setting unrealistic objectives can be unpleasant and demotivating, even though ambition is vital. When defining goals, take into account the time, talents, and resources you have at your disposal. Setting a challenge for yourself is essential, but it must be a task you can meet. Divide your objective into more manageable, realistic stages if it feels overwhelming or unattainable. In this manner, you can keep moving forward toward your ultimate goal while also celebrating tiny triumphs along the way.

Your objectives should also be pertinent to your broader aims and ideals. Align your objectives with your long-term vision by taking into account the wider picture of your life. Make sure the objectives you establish will help you improve personally or professionally and are significant to you. You'll strive toward your goals with greater drive and enjoyment if you stay true to what matters most to you.

Finally, objectives should have a deadline. Setting deadlines makes you feel more urgent and you in prioritizing your work. Without a set deadline, objectives frequently get postponed indefinitely, resulting in lack of action and stagnation. Divide your major objectives into more manageable steps with due dates for each. This not only keeps you on course, but it also enables you to change your tactics as necessary.

You get the ability to convert your ideals into workable action plans by setting SMART goals. It gives you a clear path forward, boosting your chances of success.

Keep in mind that success involves more than just achieving the ultimate result; it also involves the process of growth and development along the way. Accept the power of SMART objectives and discover the keys to your own success.

2.2 CREATING AN ACTION PLAN

Success is a goal that many people strive for, yet it frequently eludes them because of poor planning and lack of direction. One needs to have a clear action plan in order to discover the keys to success. This strategy acts as a road map for reaching objectives and coming true to dreams. Individuals can achieve clarity and generate momentum to realize their dreams by adhering to five essential stages.

1. *Define Your Vision:* Having a clear idea of what you want to accomplish is the first step toward success. Ask yourself at first, "What does success mean to me?" Set SMART goals that are precise, measurable, achievable, relevant, and time-bound and that reflect your values and aspirations. A clearly defined vision creates the framework for your goals, whether they are related to your personal development, professional success, or financial security.

2. *Divide it into goals:* After you have a clear vision, divide it into more achievable, smaller goals. These achievements will serve as stepping stones to help you reach your final objective, making the road less intimidating. Establish the steps or sub-goals needed to complete each milestone. You may keep your motivation up and measure your progress more precisely by concentrating on one milestone at a time.

3. *Identify Resources and Skills:* Consider the tools and knowledge required to reach your objectives. Determine the information, skills, networks, or expertise needed to advance. Developing a support system or seeking mentors or experts are a few examples of how to do this. Your chances of success will increase if you are conscious of your weaknesses and actively look for answers or help.

4. Set priorities and make plans: Successful time management is essential. Set your tasks in order of importance and make a detailed strategy. Organize your goals into manageable chunks, and give each one a reasonable deadline. Set due dates. Regularly assess your progress and, if required, make changes. Remember that flexibility is key, and your strategy should provide adjustment in response to shifting conditions.

5. Take Consistent Action: Success demands constant work and consistency; it cannot be attained overnight. Make a commitment to consistently pursuing your goals, even if it just requires a few tiny steps every day. Creating positive routines and habits can help you preserve your strength, tenacity, and ability to succeed.

6. Assess, evaluate, and decide on your action plan: A strategy is required. Consider the job you've done and use critical thinking. Insights gained from mentors, peers, or experts can improve action. Make a success strategy. A plan of action is essential for this trip. By influencing yourself, working hard, and being motivated, the first, most gratifying way to stay motivated to reach your goals is to visualize accomplishment. Maintaining an optimistic outlook on your development will keep you inspired when faced with difficulties.

In conclusion, taking action is essential to discovering the keys to success. Individuals may find their way to attaining their objectives by having a clear vision, well-defined milestones, and a planned strategy. Success may be attained through taking persistent action, assessing results, and remaining motivated. Keep in mind that while the road to success may include ups and downs, sticking to your action plan will get you there in the end.

2.3 OVERCOMING OBSTACLES AND STAYING COMMITTED

When seeking success, overcoming challenges and maintaining commitment are crucial. We frequently face obstacles and failures on the path to accomplishing our goals. However, how we respond to and get through these challenges ultimately decides how successful we are. Our mental fortitude, resilience, and determination hold the key to conquering challenges and maintaining our commitment.

Having a development attitude is one of the most important aspects of overcoming challenges. With a growth mindset, we may see challenges as opportunities for development and learning rather than as impediments. People with a growth mindset recognize that obstacles offer an opportunity to learn new skills, information, and experiences rather than becoming demotivated by failures. They face challenges with positivity and confidence in their capacity to adapt and succeed.

Another essential quality to overcome challenges and maintain commitment is resilience. People who are resilient have the capacity to overcome challenges. They realize that obstacles are a necessary part of the path and that failure doesn't diminish their value or chances of achievement. By developing resilience, we strengthen our ability to endure adversity and keep our dedication to attaining our objectives.

Furthermore, perseverance is crucial in the pursuit of achievement. Dedication, attention, and the desire to do the required effort are requirements for commitment. When faced with obstacles, it is simple to lose motivation or to feel like giving up when progress seems to be taking too long. However, being committed implies remaining steadfast in our resolve and faithful to our objectives.

Accountability may also be extremely important for conquering challenges and maintaining commitment. Sharing our objectives and achievements with others can provide us the motivation and support we need to keep going. Having accountability may help us stay dedicated and motivated even through difficult times, whether it's by finding a mentor, joining a group of like-minded people, or just confiding in a trusted friend.

The key to success is not only in our capacity for overcoming challenges, but also in our tenacity in sticking with our course of action. We may overcome challenges and find success by creating a growth attitude, adopting resilience, being accountable, and retaining commitment. Remember that while the road to success may not always be straight, with the correct attitude, patience, and dedication, we can conquer any challenge that stands in our way.

Chapter 3

DEVELOPING A GROWTH MINDSET:

EMBRACING CHALLENGES AND LEARNING FROM FAILURES

The road to success is frequently paved with obstacles, setbacks, and failures. But what distinguishes the successful from the others is their capacity to cultivate a development mentality. They are aware that obstacles and setbacks are actually chances for development and learning rather than obstacles.

The idea that intelligence and skills may be increased through hard work, perseverance, and a willingness to learn is known as a growth mindset. By adopting this perspective, people are empowered to see obstacles and setbacks as stepping stones to achievement rather than as proof of their fundamental limits.

So what are the keys to embracing challenges and having a development mindset?

First and foremost, it's important to accept the idea of deliberate practice. This entails actively looking for chances to step outside of your comfort zone and pushing yourself to do better. You may learn new talents and improve as a person by immersing yourself in difficult work. The practice of accepting problems rather than avoiding those helps you succeed.

Second, it's crucial to reframe setbacks as teachable moments. Successful people perceive mistakes as chances for development and transformation rather than as irreversible losses. They are aware that failure offers insightful feedback by revealing potential development areas. Failures become stepping stones on the path to success through assessing, learning from, and adjusting past mistakes.

Furthermore, a growth mindset's key component is gaining resilience. Successful people are aware that obstacles are a necessary component of the path to success. They keep a positive outlook and use these experiences as fuel to move forward after failures, setbacks, and rejections. When resilience and a growth mindset are combined, people may persevere in the face of difficulty and conquer challenges with tenacity.

Seeking out constructive criticism and taking advice from others is another key to success. People with a growth mindset foster an environment of ongoing learning by surrounding themselves with people who challenge and encourage them. They aggressively seek feedback on their performance, which enables them to spot problem areas and make the required corrections. Learning from the experiences and knowledge of others offers priceless insights and hastens personal development.

Setting both short-term and long-term goals is also essential. Stay motivated, concentrated, and provide a clear growth mentality and pattern to advance your goals. And by setting attainable objectives, people with a growth mindset face fewer obstacles and guarantee long-term development that needs work to learn and advance. People unlock success by taking on obstacles, developing resilience, and asking for feedback. Understanding is only a byproduct of greater human development.

3.1 UNDERSTANDING THE DIFFERENCE BETWEEN A FIXED MINDSET AND GROWTH MINDSET

Our path to success is significantly influenced by how we see our capabilities and tackle problems. A person's potential for success is greatly influenced by their attitude, particularly whether it is fixed or growth-oriented. The key to success may be found in knowing how these two mindsets vary from one another and the secrets they each carry.

The core tenet of a fixed mentality is the idea that intellect, ability, and aptitude are fixed attributes that are predetermined from birth. People with fixed mindsets frequently believe that their abilities are inherent and immutable. They frequently avoid tasks out of a fear of failing and facing criticism.

Therefore, instead of moving outside of their comfort zones to explore new chances, individuals can choose to continue with what they are familiar with. Since they believe talents should come naturally or not at all, these people see effort as pointless.

A growth mindset, on the other hand, is based on the idea that abilities and intellect can be improved through commitment, effort, and practice. People who adopt a development mindset see obstacles as chances for improvement and failures as instructive experiences. They accept the idea of constant development and are aware that patience and hard effort are necessary for success. People who have a development mentality are more willing to take chances, seek feedback, and keep going when things become tough.

The contrast between these two attitudes holds the keys to success. A growth mentality spurs progress and opens doors to new opportunities, whereas a fixed attitude restricts one's potential and hinders personal development. Here are a few essential strategies for using a growth mindset to achieve success:

1. Accept difficulties: Accept challenges totally rather than avoiding them out of a fear of failure or disgrace. Opportunities for skill development and personal improvement are presented by challenges. Recognize that setbacks and errors are inevitable components of the learning process and stepping stones to achievement.

2. Develop a love of learning: Develop a passion for lifelong learning and development. Look for information and abilities outside of your comfort zone. Encourage yourself to learn new skills and maintain your curiosity about the world. Developing a love of studying can open up countless opportunities for both career and personal development.

3. Stress effort and perseverance: Recognize that success is frequently the product of hard work and dedication rather than just natural talent. Develop a strong work ethic, recognize the worth of your efforts, and keep going despite obstacles. Keep in mind that progress is made incrementally, and this is the key to long-term success.

4. Accept failure as a learning opportunity:
Reframe failure from a setback to an opportunity to improve and learn. Analyze your mistakes, draw insightful conclusions from them, and use those conclusions to guide your future actions. When failure is seen from the perspective of a development mindset, it turns into a stepping stone toward success.

5. Seek input and work together: View
constructive criticism as a chance for improvement. Ask for advice from mentors, peers, and subject-matter experts on a regular basis. Engage in cooperative activities and surround yourself with people who will push you to new heights. You may quicken the process of your personal development and success by making use of the collective wisdom and experiences of others.

In conclusion, knowing the distinction between a fixed mentality and a growing mindset is the key to learning the success techniques. You may advance your personal and professional progress by developing a growth mindset, accepting difficulties, appreciating work and tenacity, viewing failure as a teaching moment, and asking for feedback. Keep in mind that when you approach life with the perspective of constant development and progress, success is not preset or limited—it is within grasp.

3.2 CULTIVATING A GROWTH MINDSET

Cultivating a development attitude is crucial for success in both personal and professional undertakings. A growth mindset is the conviction that aptitudes, skills, and talents can be enhanced and developed with commitment, effort, and a willingness to learn. One's actual potential is unlocked by adopting this mentality, which also promotes resilience, flexibility, and the capacity to get beyond challenges. The keys to developing a growth mindset are accepting failure as a learning opportunity, appreciating effort, seeking feedback, and embracing difficulties.

1. Embrace problems: People with a development mindset actively seek out new and challenging projects rather than avoiding problems. They are aware that obstacles present chances for development, learning, and advancement. By taking on obstacles head-on, students grow their knowledge, learn new talents, and become more confident in their abilities. Accepting obstacles fosters optimism and the conviction that success is possible with hard work and determination.

2. Value work: People with a development mindset understand how important work is to success. It acknowledges that perseverance, commitment, and persistent effort are essential components for development and improvement. People with a growth mindset are aware that success depends more on their desire to invest the time and effort needed to perfect a skill than it does on their natural aptitude or talents. By emphasizing effort, one develops grit, resilience, and a willingness to keep going in the face of challenges.

3. Ask for Feedback: A key tool for improvement and development is feedback. People that have a development mentality aggressively seek out criticism from others and see it as a chance to progress. They are open to constructive criticism because they see it as useful knowledge that may point out their weaknesses and help them hone their abilities. Individuals may improve their strategies, fix errors, and quicken their achievements by accepting feedback.

4. Accept Failure as a Learning Opportunity: Failure is a part of life that is unavoidable, but how we see and handle it determines our perspective. People with a growth mentality see failure as a learning opportunity rather than seeing it as a setback or a reflection on their value. They recognize that failures and errors are stepping stones to success and regard them as priceless lessons that offer knowledge and feedback for development. By changing the way they view failure, people may recover more quickly, learn from their errors, and ultimately succeed more.

5. Develop a Love of Learning: A growth mindset depends on a passion for education and an eagerness to discover new opportunities. People who have a growth mentality approach life with the mindset of a student, always seeking out information, picking up new skills, and broadening their perspectives. They are conscious of the fact that learning is a lifetime endeavor and that there is always opportunity for development. One may stay flexible, open to new ideas, and better able to negotiate the intricacies of a constantly changing environment by nurturing a passion of learning.

Finally, developing a development mentality is essential for success. People may realize their full potential and develop the attitudes and abilities necessary to overcome barriers in their road to success by accepting challenges, appreciating work, seeking feedback, and viewing failure as a learning opportunity. It's important to keep in mind that success isn't fixed or predetermined; rather, it comes from tenacity, hard effort, and a mindset focused on expansion and ongoing improvement of oneself.

3.3 EMBRACING CHALLENGES AND VIEWING FAILURES AS LEARNING OPPORTUNITIES

Sure! The key to success is accepting difficulties and seeing setbacks as teaching experiences. Many prosperous people and organizations are aware that setbacks and challenges are not impediments to be avoided, but rather steppingstones on the route to achievement. Achieving amazing success in one's pursuits is possible for anybody who adopts a mentality that views obstacles as chances for personal development and failures as instructive lessons.

Changing our perspective on obstacles is one of the first steps toward accepting them. We should consider difficulties as chances to stretch ourselves beyond our comfort zones, learn new skills, and get over restrictions rather than as burdens or hurdles.

Challenges put our skills to the test and push us to create, adapt, and come up with original answers. They open doors for personal development, empowering us to develop greater resiliency, confidence, and resourcefulness.

Furthermore, mistakes should be viewed as chances for growth rather than causes for despair. Having a development mentality that views losses as transitory setbacks rather than permanent defeats and useful lessons is necessary for accepting failure. Failures provide us the opportunity to reflect on what went wrong, pinpoint problem areas, and create successful tactics. As long as we continue to grow and learn from each failure, we will eventually succeed.

Successful people are aware of the value of tenacity and persistence in the face of difficulties and setbacks. They learn to keep going even when things are difficult. They accept setbacks as vital stepping stones on the path to success because they are aware that great accomplishments demand commitment, perseverance, hard effort, and the ability to overcome obstacles.

Additionally, embracing difficulties and seeing setbacks as learning opportunities may be tremendously aided by surrounding ourselves with a strong network of people who share our perspective. Having mentors, coaches, or like-minded peers may offer support, direction, and other viewpoints. They can guide us through trying situations and offer insightful advice that will help us continue to learn and develop from every encounter.

In the end, adopting a mindset that embraces difficulties and sees mistakes as teaching moments can result in extraordinary achievement. When we adopt a development mindset and alter our viewpoint, obstacles become stepping stones and mistakes teach us valuable lessons. We may reach our full potential and open the door to higher accomplishments by consistently seeking out challenges, learning from setbacks, persevering, and leaning on a supporting network. Success comes from accepting obstacles totally and using setbacks as stepping stones on the path to greatness, not from avoiding them.

Chapter 4

BUILDING RESILIENCE:

BOUNCING BACK FROM SETBACKS

Building resilience is a crucial ability that enables people to recover from failures and conquer obstacles they face throughout their life. Even while the road to achievement may appear clear-cut, obstacles will inevitably arise. However, the capacity to overcome these obstacles and navigate through failures is what distinguishes successful people from others.

A growth attitude is one of the keys to enhancing resilience. The idea that one's skills and intellect can be grown via commitment and effort is one that was made popular by psychologist Carol Decks. Adopting a growth mindset enables people to see losses as chances for growth and learning rather than as failures. It motivates people to persevere in the face of difficulties, cultivates a positive mindset, and eventually leads to the skills necessary for success.

The development of a robust support network is another essential strategy for boosting resilience. Being around by upbeat and encouraging people may significantly impact how one handles adversity. When self-doubt strikes, these people may give a sympathetic ear, advice, and a gentle reminder of one's talents and qualities. Additionally, having a strong support network can aid in perspective-taking by providing a variety of perspectives and new ideas that may help to clarify the current issue.

People that are resilient value their health and engage in self-care. In order to keep a powerful and resilient attitude, it is essential to take care of one's physical, mental, and emotional health. One may improve their capacity to deal with setbacks by partaking in activities like exercise, meditation, and cultivating meaningful connections. Individuals are better able to handle stress and have a good perspective by emphasizing self-care.

Building resilience can also be aided by having a sense of purpose and adopting reasonable goals. People are motivated and driven even in the face of failures when they have a clear vision and a feeling of purpose. Setting realistic objectives makes sure that people position themselves for success and enables them to enjoy tiny successes along the road. This feeling of advancement and success encourages resilience and gives people the motivation to keep moving forward in the face of challenges.

Lastly recognizing failure as an intrinsic part of the path is a crucial tip to growing resilience. Resilient people perceive failure as a stepping stone toward success rather than a final result or a personal defect. They are aware that failure presents a chance to grow, adapt, and succeed. Failure is reframed in this way so that setbacks are less demoralizing and more useful learning experiences on the road to achievement.

In conclusion, success is mostly dependent on developing resilience and recovering quickly from setbacks. People may build the resilience needed to overcome every difficulty or setback they may encounter by adopting a growth mindset, establishing a strong support system, prioritizing self-care, setting realistic objectives, and embracing failure. Keep in mind that failures are not obstacles to overcome, but rather chances for development and eventual success.

4.1 UNDERSTANDING RESILIENCE AND ITS IMPORTANCE

A significant quality that is essential to success and overcoming obstacles is resilience. It describes a person's capacity to recover from failures, adapt to change, and keep an optimistic outlook in the face of difficulty. People who are resilient have the mental and emotional fortitude to deal with life's ups and downs, eventually enabling them to achieve their objectives.

Understanding resilience and appreciating its significance in all spheres of life is one of the keys to success. Resilience functions as a driving force that encourages people to pursue their goals, whether they be in personal relationships, job objectives, or general well-being. Here are some important details about the success principles that come from knowing and practicing resilience:

1. Accepting hurdles as Opportunities for Growth: People who are resilient see hurdles as teaching opportunities rather than impassable barriers. They accept that obstacles are a necessary part of the path and see them as opportunities for both professional and personal development. They may learn important lessons from mistakes and apply them to improve their abilities and tactics by adopting this approach.

2. Developing a Positive Attitude: A resilient person maintains their optimism despite hardship. They realize that keeping a positive outlook gives them the ability to respond to difficulties with ingenuity and tenacity. This mentality enables them to stay motivated, solution-focused, and concentrated, which enables them to conquer problems more successfully.

3. *Creating a Strong Support System:* Resilience flourishes in a strong system. Resilient people recognize the value of surrounding themselves with a network of loved ones, friends, mentors, and coworkers who can offer them support, encouragement, and emotional direction. This support network acts as a safety net during trying times, enhancing their self-esteem and assisting them in maintaining their path to success.

4. *Developing Emotional Intelligence:* People who are resilient have high emotional intelligence, which allows them to comprehend and successfully control their emotions. In trying circumstances, they are able to control their emotional reactions, which helps them think more clearly and make better judgments. They retain a balanced viewpoint and foster good connections through practicing emotional intelligence, both of which support their overall success and resilience.

5. *Engaging in Self-Care:* Self-care and resilience go hand in hand. Resilience is higher in those who put their physical and mental health first. People can develop the resilience necessary to overcome obstacles in their way to success by engaging in activities like exercise, mindfulness, proper rest, and healthy relationships.

6. Retaining Flexibility and Adaptability: People who are resilient have a mentality that is both flexible and adaptive. They are aware that situations might change and that life is unpredictable. They are more able to adapt their plans and tactics by staying open to new concepts, viewpoints, and possibilities. Due to their adaptability, they may change course as necessary and pursue several successful avenues.

In conclusion, the keys to success in a variety of fields lay in resilience. Individuals may develop the mental and emotional fortitude required to face problems head-on, learn from setbacks, and continue in pursuit of their objectives by recognizing and encouraging resilience. Resilient people retain an optimistic outlook, develop emotional intelligence, cultivate a supporting network, practice self-care, and stay adaptive and flexible while welcoming setbacks as chances for growth. Understanding resilience and its significance ultimately enables people to reach their full potential and succeed even in the face of difficulty.

4.2 STRATEGIES FOR BUILDING RESILIENCE

Resilience is the capacity to overcome obstacles, negotiate difficulties, and adjust to failures. Success in both the personal and professional spheres depends on it. We all undoubtedly encounter unanticipated challenges and setbacks at some time in our lives, therefore developing resilience is crucial. But the good news is that you can improve and build your resilience skills. We will look at several techniques for fostering resilience and learn the keys to success in this book.

1. Develop a growth mentality: A growth mindset is the conviction that our skills and attributes can be improved with commitment and effort. Adopting a growth mindset enables us to see challenges as chances for development and learning. It encourages us to continue despite difficulties and makes it easier for us to see failures as transitory. We may strengthen our resilience and realize our maximum potential for success by adopting a growth mindset.

2. Create Effective Support Networks: Having a network of encouraging and supporting people around you is essential for developing resilience. When dealing with challenging events, these people can offer emotional support, advice, and diverse viewpoints. You may stay grounded and gain the fortitude required to endure through difficult circumstances by establishing connections with like-minded people, mentors, friends, or support groups.

3. Engage in Self-Care: Developing resilience requires taking good care of your physical, mental, and emotional needs. Take part in pursuits that promote your wellbeing, such as exercise, meditation, time spent in nature, or hobbies. Make self-care a priority to make sure you have the strength and emotional stability to face challenges and overcome disappointments.

4. Establish Realistic objectives: Setting realistic objectives will help you feel like you have a direction and a purpose. Break down more ambitious goals into more manageable chunks, and acknowledge your accomplishments as you go. Setting achievable objectives can boost your odds of achievement and decrease your danger of being overwhelmed. This strategy helps you retain concentration and change your tactics as needed, which helps you develop resilience.

5. Improve Problem-Solving Techniques: Resilience is significantly influenced by good problem-solving abilities. When faced with difficulties, be proactive and consider viable solutions. Organize potential solutions and divide the issue into manageable components. Adopt a flexible outlook and be receptive to various strategies. You can face challenges head-on and come up with innovative solutions when you have this problem-solving approach.

6. Keep a Positive Attitude: Resilience can only be developed by keeping a positive attitude. Even though it's normal to feel bad during difficult times, try to concentrate on the things you've learnt and your room for improvement. Reframing negative ideas and practicing thankfulness can help you change your perspective and develop resilience in the face of hardship.

7. Learn from Failure: Failure is a chance for growth and a stepping stone to success. Consider failure as an opportunity to learn, adapt, and get better rather than as a personal setback. By gaining the information and experience required for future success, accepting failure helps you grow resilience.

8. Seek Professional Assistance When Necessary: Developing resilience does not include taking on difficulties by yourself. Seek out expert assistance if you're having trouble coping or feeling overwhelmed. Therapists, coaches, or mentors can offer direction, support, and efficient solutions that are adapted to your particular circumstance.

Keep in mind that developing resilience requires time and effort. By implementing these techniques into your life, you may build the resilience required to overcome obstacles and accomplish your objectives. Develop a development mentality, take advantage of setbacks as learning opportunities, and surround oneself with supportive people. With resilience as your guiding principle, you will be better able to overcome challenges and realize your full potential.

4.3 CULTIVATING A POSITIVE MINDSET IN THE FACE OF ADVERSITY

In reality, one of the most important aspects of success is developing a positive outlook in the face of difficulty. An optimistic outlook may have a huge influence on our capacity to overcome difficulties, setbacks, or unforeseen barriers and pave the way for success. Here are some tips for cultivating a happy mentality, even when the path to success might occasionally seem elusive:

1. *Adopt a growth mentality:* A growth mindset is the conviction that one can acquire skills and traits through commitment, effort, and perseverance. Consider setbacks as chances for learning and progress rather than failures. By adopting a development mentality, you may perceive obstacles as stepping stones on the way to achievement.

2. Develop self-awareness: Pay attention to your feelings and thoughts, particularly when things are difficult. Recognize when unfavorable ideas enter your mind and actively choose to change them into uplifting and powerful ones. You may see negative thought patterns and actively attempt to change them to a positive viewpoint by developing self-awareness.

3. Concentrate on answers: Rather of wallowing in difficulties, turn your attention to locating answers. Ask yourself, "What can I do to improve this situation?" if you are presented with difficulty. You may empower yourself to act and bring about change by focusing your attention on seeking answers.

4. Surround Yourself with Positive People: Create a solid network of upbeat, like-minded people who will support and motivate you. Positive people may raise your mood and provide you inspiration while you're going through a tough period. Find mentors, become involved in good causes, and do things that help you grow as a person.

5. Develop an Attitude of Gratitude: Being grateful enables you to change your attention from what is going wrong to what is going good. Even in trying times, set aside some time each day to think on your blessings. Finding the positive side of things and appreciating your accomplishments, no matter how minor, may be facilitated by this discipline.

6. Look for Yourself: Self-care is essential for sustaining a good outlook. Take part in activities that will nurture your body, mind, and spirit. This might be engaging in physical activity, practicing mindfulness or meditation, spending time outside, engaging in activities you like, or just taking breaks to relax and recharge. By placing self-care first, you strengthen your resilience and general wellbeing.

7. Establish Realistic Goals: By establishing realistic objectives, you can monitor your development and recognize minor triumphs along the road. Larger goals should be broken down into more manageable chunks. Every accomplishment strengthens a positive outlook and inspires you to keep going forward.

Keep in mind that developing a good outlook requires lifelong effort. Consistent effort, self-compassion, and the ability to adjust and grow from hardship are necessary. You may discover the keys to success even in the midst of hardship by adopting a positive outlook, looking for solutions, and encouraging personal development.

Chapter 5

TIME MANAGEMENT AND PRODUCTIVITY:

MAXIMIZING YOUR EFFICIENCY AND EFFECTIVENESS

Successful time management and productivity are essential for both personal and professional success. You may considerably boost your productivity and assist in reaching your objectives by efficiently managing your time and using your resources. We will examine several important time management and productivity strategies in this post.

1. Establish Clear and Achievable objectives: Setting clear and attainable objectives is the first step in efficient time management. You can prioritize your work and manage your time effectively if you have a clear knowledge of what you want to accomplish. Make sure your objectives are SMART (specific, measurable, achievable, relevant, and time-bound).

2. Prioritize and concentrate: After deciding on your objectives, order your duties according to their urgency and significance. You'll be able to focus your time and effort on high-priority tasks as a result. Avoid multitasking since it might harm your productivity and cause mistakes. To improve concentration and productivity, concentrate on one job at a time.

3. Plan and Organize: Establish a methodical approach to time management. Make a daily or weekly plan with designated times for certain activities. Use time management tools to keep track of your projects, deadlines, and appointments, such as calendars, to-do lists, or project management applications. This will keep you on track and help you stay organized.

4. Eliminate time wasters by identifying tasks that take up a lot of time yet don't really advance your objectives: Common time wasters include overusing social media, scheduling pointless meetings, reading email excessively, and failing to delegate. Reduce or get rid of these time wasters to increase productivity.

5. Develop Your Delegation Skills: Accept That You Can't Do Everything Yourself. Give chores to capable people to free up your time for more significant obligations. In addition to empowering your team members, delegation frees you up to concentrate on tasks that call for your expertise.

6. Practice Effective Communication: Managing time and productivity requires effective communication. Give individuals a clear understanding of your expectations, time frames, and ambitions. Use tools to keep everyone in the loop and prevent misunderstandings, such as email project management software or scheduled team meetings.

7. Take pauses and Recharge: To prevent burnout and sustain productivity, take regular pauses. Small pauses during the day can improve attention, refresh your memory, and lower stress. Take use of this time to rest and recharge by doing things like going for a little stroll, practicing meditation, or listening to music.

8. Continue to learn and get better: Striking a balance between productivity and efficiency is a lifelong endeavor. Evaluate your performance frequently, pinpoint areas that need development, and look for educational opportunities. Reading books, going to seminars or workshops, or even asking mentors for advice who can share insightful advice are all possible ways to do this.

In conclusion, success requires efficient time management and productivity. Adopting these success strategies can help you achieve your objectives, increase your efficiency, and live a more balanced and satisfying life. Keep in mind that effective time management and setting priorities are the keys to success.

5.1 THE IMPORTANCE OF TIME MANAGEMENT

Time is a finite resource that is shared equitably among all people. However, what distinguishes successful people from others is their capacity to efficiently manage and maximize every minute. A crucial ability that significantly affects both personal and professional success is time management.

Understanding the value of time is one of the keys to success. Successful people understand that time is a valuable resource that cannot be replaced once lost. They are aware that every minute squandered on pointless tasks or lost to procrastination represents a lost chance for development and success. They prioritize things, establish definite goals, and put up great effort in pursuing them because they value time.

Efficiency and productivity may both be improved via effective time management. Successful people are adept at planning their workload and setting aside particular times for certain tasks. To help them keep focused and on task, they create timetables, to-do lists, or employ productivity tools. By effectively managing their time, people may finish work more quickly while avoiding interruptions and retaining a high level of focus.

Successful people may attain a healthy work-life balance by using time management. They are aware of how crucial it is to put their personal connections, health, and wellbeing above their careers. They retain a sense of fulfillment and prevent burnout by making time for family activities like exercise and leisure. Their success and happiness as a whole are a result of their balanced approach to time management.

Additionally, efficient time management enhances decision-making. People that are successful take the time to consider all of their alternatives, evaluate the advantages and disadvantages, and then decide. They are aware that making hasty judgments without giving them sufficient thought might result in errors and regret. By effectively using their time, they free up time for thought, analysis, and assessment, which enables them to make decisions that will help them succeed.

Additionally, time management fosters self-control and motivation. Successful people follow their schedules, fulfill deadlines, and keep their word. They are aware that desire, perseverance, and consistency are necessary for success. By properly managing their time, people build a solid work ethic and the discipline to stick to their plans and ambitions.

Effective time management also lowers stress and enhances general wellbeing. Tasks are prioritized, broken down into manageable portions, and realistic deadlines are set by successful people. By doing this, they stay ahead of last-minute rushes, do away with the need for extended workdays, and feel in control of their schedules. They can concentrate on their objectives with a clear and peaceful mind thanks to this control's reduction of stress levels.

Mastering time management is crucial to discovering the keys to success. Making the most of one's few resources allows one to boost productivity and efficiency, maintain a good work-life balance, improve decision-making, foster self-control and discipline, and lessen stress.

People may unlock their full potential and achieve the success they seek by appreciating the value of time and making judicious use of it. So begin managing your time well and start appreciating how valuable it is as you go toward achievement.

5.2 EFFECTIVE TECHNIQUE FOR PRIORITIZING AND MANAGING YOUR TIME

Time has become a valuable and finite resource in the fast-paced world of today. It's essential to develop the ability of time management and good prioritization if you want to succeed. You may unlock your potential and achieve more than you ever imagined possible by boosting productivity and eliminating distractions. This article examines time management secrets and provides helpful advice on how to effectively prioritize your work.

1. Set Specific Goals:

Setting clear and precise goals is the first step towards time management success. Establish your long-term goals first, and then divide them into more manageable, achievable tasks. These objectives serve as a road map to keep you on track while you prioritize your chores and maintain concentration. Keep in mind that objectives should be specific, time-bound, and quantifiable.

2. Priorities your task:

Prioritizing your duties is crucial after you've established your goals. A well-known method for classifying jobs into four quadrants is the Eisenhower Matrix: important and urgent, important but not urgent, not important but urgent, and not important and not urgent. By identifying and doing the most important things first, this strategy helps you avoid wasting time on unimportant chores.

3. Compile a to-do-list:

Making use of a to-do list is essential for time management. Make a list of the things that need to get done each day before you get started. To keep focused and organized throughout the day, follow this list. For the purpose of fostering a feeling of urgency and preventing procrastination, think about giving each task a deadline. Check off each item on your list as you finish it to feel accomplished.

4. Employ the time-blocking method:

Scheduling particular time blocks for various activities is known as time blocking, and it is an effective method. Set out separate time slots for duties like email replying, meetings, creative work, and personal hobbies. You may get rid of uncertainty and interruptions by creating a day's worth of plans in advance. Keep in mind that it is essential to keep your allotted blocks uninterrupted and to maintain your discipline.

5. Discover How to Delegate:

Knowing when to assign duties to others is one of the keys to good time management. Your burden will be reduced via delegation, and you'll have more time to devote to high-value tasks. Determine which duties may be delegated to coworkers or subordinates if they have the necessary knowledge and experience. Effective delegating encourages productivity and team expansion.

6. Exercise Batching Time:

The process of collecting related jobs and allocating certain blocks of time to finish them all at once is known as time batching. For instance, set aside a certain period each day to manage emails rather than checking them frequently. Similar activities can be batch-processed to minimize the need to switch contexts often, improving focus and efficiency.

7. Keep distracted:

One of the biggest time wasters is distraction. To keep your attention, it's important to recognize them and successfully handle them. By disabling unnecessary notifications, keeping your workplace orderly, and establishing boundaries with family members and coworkers, you may reduce distractions. Use applications or productivity tools that can keep you focused and reduce distractions.

Effective time management is the key to success in every effort, to sum up. By putting these useful strategies into practice, you can take control of your time, increase productivity, and accomplish your goals. Always set specific objectives. Create To-do lists, and put in order time blocking, efficient delegation, time batching, and distraction management as recommended. You may build effective time management skills that can boost your overall performance with effort and practice.

5.3 REDUCE DISTRACTION AND IMPROVE FOCUS

Successfully limiting distractions and enhancing attention are the keys to success. Distractions abound in today's fast-paced environment, making it harder and harder to maintain focus on our objectives and find the success we want. However, we may improve our capacity to focus and make the most of our time and energy by employing certain tactics and taking a disciplined approach. Here are some pointers to assist you in perfecting the skill of reducing distraction and increasing focus:

1. Establish a distraction-free environment: Begin by establishing a distraction-free workstation or study location. Clear your workspace of any extraneous items that can distract you and arrange your surroundings to encourage concentration. To reduce outside noise, you may also think about using noise-canceling headphones or ambient noise applications.

2. Establish priorities and goals that are in line with your long-term vision: Clearly describe your priorities and create targets. Understanding what is most important to you will make it simpler to weed out distractions that don't advance your achievement. Learn to say no to projects or obligations that are not in line with your goals and learn to focus your time and energy on activities that move you closer to your objectives.

3. Divide big, intimidating chores into smaller, more manageable ones: Distractions may thrive in large, overwhelming projects. Divide them into smaller, easier-to-manage activities. This will enable you to approach them step-by-step while ensuring that your attention is sustained. In order to stay motivated and on track, celebrate minor accomplishments along the road.

4. Develop a mindfulness and meditation practice: Developing a mindfulness and meditation practice may greatly improve your capacity to concentrate. With the use of these techniques, you may teach your mind to put distracting ideas aside and focus instead on the here and now. To improve your capacity to concentrate, schedule frequent mindfulness or meditation sessions into your schedule.

5. Adopt time management strategies: Using efficient time management tactics helps keep you organized and reduce pointless distractions. Investigate methods like the Pomodoro Technique, in which you work for concentrated intervals of 25 minutes, followed by brief breaks. By providing small breaks from work while retaining a laser-like focus when working, this technique can increase productivity.

6. Use technology wisely: When it comes to distractions, technology may be a double-edged sword. It has the potential to be both a potent instrument for productivity and a persistent source of disruption. Set limits on how much time you spend on technology by disabling notifications or utilizing productivity tools that prevent distracting websites and apps when you're working or studying.

7. Take care of your physical and mental health:
Your capacity for concentration is highly correlated with your state of general health. Prioritize your own well-being by getting enough sleep, eating wholesome foods, and exercising frequently. You'll have the energy and mental clarity required to maintain concentration and succeed if you take care of your physical and mental health.

Focusing more and minimizing distractions is a lifetime exercise that calls for continual effort and self-control. You'll discover that when you master these abilities and adopt the aforementioned habits, you'll be more successful in every aspect of your life and be able to get closer to your goals with greater ease. Keep in mind that success requires more than simply hard effort; it also requires smart work and staying focus on what matters most.

Chapter 6

CONTINUOUS LEARNING AND PERSONAL GROWTH: EXPANDING YOUR KNOWLEDGE AND SKILLS

The secret to success and reaching your goals is constant learning and personal development. It is crucial to keep learning and growing in the fast-paced, always changing world of today. Continuous learning makes you stand out from the competition and helps you achieve better success in both your professional and personal lives.

Learning new information, whether through formal schooling, workshops, seminars, or online courses, is one of the keys to success. It entails a desire to learn more and a constant drive to advance your knowledge and abilities. You can remain ahead of the curve and adjust to quickly evolving industries and technology thanks to your dedication to learning.

Additionally, learning new information is simply one aspect of personal progress; it also entails developing and refining a variety of talents. It can involve developing your interpersonal and communication skills, strengthening your capacity for critical thought, or learning new technologies that are pertinent to your line of work. You may boost your worth to potential employers, clients, and coworkers by consistently developing and improving these talents. This thus creates more prospects for achievement and professional progression.

Taking an active role in your own development is another key to success. Take the initiative to seek out possibilities rather than waiting for them to come to you. Seek for opportunities to use your newly acquired knowledge and abilities in practical settings. This can entail taking on new duties, volunteering for difficult initiatives, or working on side projects that take you beyond of your comfort zone. Being proactive shows that you are committed to your own personal development and ongoing learning, which positions you for greater success.

Furthermore, technical proficiency and subject matter understanding are not the only requirements for success. Strong interpersonal interactions and emotional intelligence development are also essential components of personal development. Place a strong emphasis on developing active listening, good communication, and empathy. These skills let you relate to and comprehend others more deeply, which promotes cooperation and teamwork.

To sum up, long-term success depends on ongoing learning and personal development. You put yourself in a position for greater possibilities and successes by adopting a growth mindset and actively seeking out new information and abilities. Keep in mind that success is a journey rather than a destination, and the road to success is paved with a dedication to lifelong learning and personal development.

6.1 LIFELONG LEARNING AND ITS BENEFIT

The process of continuously gaining information and skills throughout the course of a person's life is called lifelong learning. It includes a range of learning activities, such as informal learning, self-directed learning, and professional development, and goes beyond formal schooling. In the quickly evolving world of today, where new technologies, industries, and ideas are always emerging, lifelong learning has become more and more important.

The contribution that lifelong learning makes to one's own personal development and progress is one of its main advantages. People may improve their understanding of the world, develop critical thinking skills, and widen their viewpoints by continually learning new things.

The process of continuously gaining information and skills throughout the course of a person's life is called lifelong learning. It includes a range of learning activities, such as informal learning, self-directed learning, and professional development, and goes beyond formal schooling. In the quickly evolving world of today, where new technologies, industries, and ideas are always emerging, lifelong learning has become more and more important.

The contribution that lifelong learning makes to one's own personal development and progress is one of its main advantages. People may improve their understanding of the world, develop critical thinking skills, and widen their viewpoints by continually learning new things. Individuals that embrace a philosophy of continual learning may help to create good change in their industries and inspire innovation within their enterprises.

Another advantage of lifelong learning is that it improves personal well-being and contentment. Participating in learning activities fosters personal fulfillment and a sense of success. As individuals overcome problems and achieve their learning objectives, they gain self-confidence and self-esteem. Lifelong learners have greater mental and emotional well-being because learning may be used to relieve stress and excite the intellect.

Furthermore, lifelong learning allows people to adapt to changing situations and overcome challenges. Individuals grow more resilient and more able to tackle problems by constantly extending their knowledge and abilities. They strengthen their problem-solving abilities, decision-making talents, and capacity to manage difficult circumstances efficiently.

Finally, lifelong learning is not only advantageous but also necessary for personal and professional success. It allows people to adapt to a changing world, improve their abilities, stimulate creativity, and enrich their lives. Individuals who embrace lifelong learning are better able to stay relevant in their jobs, grab new opportunities, and achieve personal growth and fulfillment. It is a strong instrument that may help to long-term success and a more successful and happier existence.

6.2 PURSUING PERSONAL GROWTH OPPORTUNITIES

Success is something that many people strive for. We all desire to experience development and improvement in our professions, relationships, and personal lives. While success may appear elusive and unique to each individual, there are some secrets that can open the door to personal development. Pursuing personal development opportunities is an important element in the recipe for success. Here are some insights on success secrets and how to capitalize on personal growth possibilities.

1. Develop a Growth attitude: The first key to success is to develop a growth attitude. This mentality involves having faith in one's potential to grow and improve via hard work, perseverance, and learning from mistakes. By adopting a growth mindset, you recognize that success is not exclusively decided by intrinsic aptitude, but rather by effort and ongoing personal improvement.

2. Establish Specific Goals: Having a clear vision of what you want to achieve is critical for personal development. Set precise, measurable, attainable, relevant, and time-bound (SMART) goals that correspond to your ambitions. These objectives serve as checkpoints along the way, providing you with a clear path to victory. To keep focused and motivated, evaluate and adjust your goals on a regular basis.

3. Learn Constantly: A passion for information and a dedication to constant learning are essential for personal development. Use every chance to broaden your knowledge and abilities. Reading books, attending seminars or workshops, taking online courses, or seeking mentoring from experienced persons are all examples of activities that might be included. Investing in your personal development via education helps you to remain versatile and ahead of the curve in an ever-changing environment.

4. Step Outside Your Comfort Zone: We frequently grow when we push past our comfort zones and explore into uncharted terrain. Be prepared to take measured chances and accept new challenges. Stepping outside of your comfort zone exposes you to new experiences, helps you develop resilience, and reveals hidden abilities and strengths. Instead of being afraid of failure, accept it as a stepping stone to achievement.

5. Build a Supportive Network: Surround yourself with positive, like-minded people who share your goals. A solid support system may offer advice, encouragement, and accountability. Engage with individuals who inspire and challenge you, and be willing to take guidance and critical comments. Collaboration not only improves your own progress but also opens up prospects for communal accomplishment.

6. Practice Self-Reflection: Take regular breaks to reflect on your accomplishments and opportunities for growth. Self-reflection allows you to become more self-aware, evaluate your strengths and limitations, and make required changes to your behaviors and mentality. It also enables you to celebrate your achievements along the way, which provides inspiration and a sense of accomplishment.

7. Maintain Resilience and Persistence: Success is rarely a straight line. It takes perseverance and the capacity to recover from setbacks and disappointments. Recognize that difficulties and problems are a normal component of growth and should be seen as chances for learning and progress. Cultivate persistence by being focused on your goals and never losing sight of your vision.

To summarize, pursuing personal growth opportunities is a critical component of success. You may uncover the secrets of success by adopting a growth mindset, making clear goals, constantly learning, pushing outside your comfort zone, building a supporting network, practicing self-reflection, and retaining resilience and tenacity. Remember that success is a lifetime endeavor, and personal development is the key that unlocks doors to unlimited possibilities.

6.3 DEVELOPING A HABIT OF CONTINUOUS LEARNING

One of the keys to success in life is to develop a habit of continual learning. In a fast changing world where new knowledge and technology emerge at an unprecedented rate, people who adopt a lifelong learning attitude are better positioned to adapt, grow, and prosper.

So, how can one develop the habit of continual learning? Here are some crucial methods to consider:

1. Adopt a Growth Mindset: A growth mindset is necessary for building a habit of continual learning. It entails believing that talents and intellect, rather than being fixed attributes, may be acquired through practice and effort. When you consider problems as growth opportunities, you are more inclined to seek out new information and abilities.

2. Establish Learning Objectives: In order to make continuous learning a habit, it is necessary to establish particular learning objectives. Determine where you wish to improve your knowledge or abilities. Make a plan for what you want to accomplish and divide it into smaller, more doable objectives. Setting specific goals offers concentration and drive to continue studying.

3. calendar Regular Learning Time: Make learning a priority by making time in your calendar for it. Set aside time each day or week for reading, taking online courses, attending seminars, or participating in other learning activities. Making studying a non-negotiable component of your routine can help you build a habit.

4. Investigate several Learning strategies: Because everyone has a unique learning style, it is critical to investigate several strategies that work best for you. Some people like to read books or articles, whilst others prefer to watch informative videos or listen to podcasts. Experiment with several mediums and formats to see what works best for you.

5. Discover a Learning Community: Learning does not have to be a solo endeavor. Seek out like-minded people who share your enthusiasm for lifelong learning. Participating in forums or discussion groups, as well as visiting local meetings, may give excellent possibilities for cooperation, support, and accountability.

6. Engage in Reflective Practice: Reflect on your learning experience on a regular basis to obtain insights and strengthen your knowledge. After finishing a course, reading a book, or meeting a new subject, pause to consider its significance and consequences. Reflective practice aids in the consolidation of knowledge and facilitates deeper comprehension.

7. *Apply What You Learn:* When you apply what you learn in real-world settings, it becomes more relevant and effective. Look for opportunities to put your gained knowledge or talents to work. Taking on new tasks at work, volunteering for initiatives relating to your learning interests, or sharing your experience with others might be examples of this.

8. *Maintain Curiosity:* Develop a feeling of curiosity and a desire for inquiry. Maintain an open mind to new ideas, opinions, and experiences. Seek out knowledge from a variety of sources and actively seek out opportunities to learn in unexpected places. Curiosity drives ongoing learning and makes the path interesting and rewarding.

Remember that cultivating a habit of continual learning is a lifetime endeavor. It takes commitment, discipline, and a desire to improve. By committing to continuous learning, you position yourself for success by keeping ahead of the curve, adjusting to change, and grabbing new possibilities. So, make studying a lifelong goal to maximize your chances of success!

Chapter 7

BUILDING POSITIVE RELATIONSHIPS: NETWORKING AND COLLABORATION

Building meaningful relationships via networking and cooperation is essential for personal and professional success. These connections may open doors, provide assistance, and offer vital chances for growth and development. However, there are several tips for leveraging the benefits of networking and cooperation that may dramatically boost your chances of success.

1. *Genuine and Authentic Connection:* Creating genuine and authentic connections with people is the first step in developing positive relationships. This is sincerely caring for people, carefully listening to their needs, and looking for methods to help and bring value to their life. Being genuine and displaying your actual self can assist to create trust and deeper connections.

2. Give Before You Receive: Adopting an attitude of giving before getting is one of the keys to effective networking and cooperation. Instead than concentrating exclusively on what others can do for you, consider how you can help others achieve their goals. Giving without expecting immediate rewards creates trust and positions you as a useful link, whether it's providing resources, delivering insights, or making introductions.

3. Be Proactive and Engaged: A passive attitude to networking and collaboration will provide ineffective outcomes. Instead, be proactive by actively searching out opportunities to engage with people, attend networking events, and collaborate on projects. Maintain connections through engaging in conversations, asking intelligent questions, and following up with individuals. Consistent effort is essential in developing and maintaining healthy connections.

4. Develop a Diverse Network: Having a diverse network is vital for acquiring new perspectives, ideas, and possibilities. Develop ties with individuals from diverse sectors and backgrounds. By broadening your network, you boost your chances of discovering new possibilities, obtaining new insights, and having access to a wider range of resources.

5. *Be Reliable and Follow Through:* Trust is the foundation of every successful relationship. It is critical to develop trust by being dependable and following through on commitments. Keep your commitments and deliver on your pledges. By regularly being dependable, you establish a solid reputation and become someone on whom people can rely, which strengthens your connections.

6. *Value Collaboration and Synergy:* Collaboration is a key success strategy. Look for ways to work with others while maximizing each other's talents and knowledge. When you combine your abilities with those of others, you may frequently produce more substantial results than if you worked alone. Keep an open mind to fresh ideas. To maximize the potential of collaboration, respect the diversity of viewpoints and establish an environment of mutual cooperation.

7. *Be a Connector and Facilitator:* Becoming a connector and facilitator within your network is another key to developing strong relationships. Introduce persons who can benefit from each other's knowledge, organize networking events, or start joint initiatives. You establish yourself as a valued resource inside your network by actively bringing people together and producing value for others.

8. *Maintain Long-Term Relationships:* Developing positive relationships is a continuous process. It must be nurtured and maintained on a regular basis. Maintain contact with your contacts, check in on their progress, and give assistance as required. Celebrate their accomplishments and milestones, and be there for them at difficult times. When you continuously invest in your connections, they will develop and bring long-term advantages.

Finally, developing favorable relationships via networking and cooperation is critical to success. You may build a strong network that supports and promotes your personal and professional progress by cultivating real connections, being proactive in giving before receiving, and embracing cooperation. Remember that the actual power of networking is found in the value you provide to others and the long-term connections you build.

7.1 THE POWER OF RELATIONSHIP IN SUCCESS

Success is frequently viewed as a personal journey motivated by personal desire and determination. While individual work and qualities are important, the importance of connections should never be ignored. Making and developing meaningful connections may help you achieve success in both your professional and personal efforts.

1. Collaboration and Synergy: Success is rarely attained alone. Building solid relationships enables cooperation and the integration of varied viewpoints, talents, and experiences. Individuals may produce novel ideas, solve challenging issues, and create synergistic benefits when they work together in a mutually supportive setting. Collective knowledge has the ability to transcend the constraints of individual thought, boosting accomplishment to new heights.

2. *Networking chances:* Relationships serve as the foundation for networking, which leads to a plethora of chances. Attending business conferences, joining professional groups, or interacting with like-minded individuals all have the potential to open up new doors to success. A large network not only gives you access to mentors, advisers, and possible clients, but it also allows you to share information resources and contacts, which may help you advance in your professional and personal development.

3. *Emotional Support:* Achieving success may be a difficult and sometimes lonely path. A strong network of trustworthy connections can give the emotional resilience required to overcome obstacles and failures. When faced with tough decisions, a network of supporting people may provide direction, encouragement, and a new viewpoint.

Their conviction in your skills may generate confidence and inspiration, allowing you to persevere during difficult situations.

4. Personal Development and Learning:

Relationships provide several chances for personal development and lifelong learning. Engaging with people from other backgrounds exposes us to fresh ideas, cultures, and ways of thinking. We can obtain insights that increase our knowledge, develop our talents, and modify our viewpoints through receiving constructive comments, mentoring, or just engaging in honest dialogues. These experiences help us grow as people, which increases our chances of success.

5. Trust and Collaboration:

Trust and mutual respect are the foundations of strong partnerships. Trust is a crucial asset in any activity because it encourages cooperation, teamwork, and long-term relationships. In a world where success is frequently dependent on collaboration with others, preserving trust becomes critical. People are more willing to interact and support those they believe in, which opens and establish genuine relationships.

Networking is more than outdoor to new possibilities and prospective collaborations.

6. *Personal Branding and Reputation:* Our personal brand and reputation are shaped by the relationships we build. Positive connections may be used to demonstrate our character, expertise, and integrity. These recommendations can boost our credibility and open doors to new opportunities. Similarly, poor relationships or a lack of genuine connections can stymie progress by instilling doubt or mistrust. Long-term success may be significantly impacted by investing in healthy connections and controlling our reputation.

Finally, success is reliant not just on individual efforts but also on the strength of connections. Making and sustaining meaningful relationships improves teamwork, opens doors to new possibilities, stimulates personal growth, and molds our personal brand and reputation. Understanding and leveraging the power of connections is a critical component in understanding success's secrets.

7.2 NETWORKING STRATEGIES AND TECHNIQUES

In today's linked society, networking methods and practices are critical to success. Building a strong network, whether you're an entrepreneur, professional, or student, may lead to new possibilities, partnerships, and information sharing. While networking may be intimidating or unsettling for some, there are success secrets that may help you navigate this process with confidence and efficacy. Consider the following essential tactics and techniques:

1. Establish a clear networking goal: Before you begin networking, establish your objectives. Determine your goals for networking, whether it's acquiring new clients, growing your expertise, or seeking new career chances. Having a defined aim will help you direct your efforts and prioritize your connections.

Merely collecting business cards or establishing social media contacts will be great. It is about developing genuine connections based on mutual benefit and trust. Spend time getting to know individuals, understanding their needs, and finding methods to help them. Remember that networking is a two-way street, so be eager to help others when feasible.

2. *Be proactive and consistent:* Networking takes time and effort. Attend relevant conferences, industry events, and networking mixers on your own initiative. Participate in online networks, forums, and social media platforms relevant to your industry. Show up on a regular basis, participate actively, and cultivate your friendships over time.

3. *Improve your communication skills:* Communication is essential in networking. Active listening is asking open-ended questions and showing genuine interest in what others have to say. Prepare to effectively define your objectives, abilities, and expertise so that you can clearly demonstrate your worth when chances come.

4. *Make use of online platforms:* In today's digital world, internet platforms may significantly improve your networking efforts. Join professional networking sites like LinkedIn and construct an engaging profile that highlights your skills and achievements. Participate in relevant groups, contribute useful knowledge, and network with people in your sector. Use technology to remain in touch with your network, such as email messaging applications and video conferencing.

5. Attend industry-specific events: Attend industry-specific events. Conferences and seminars are fantastic places to meet like-minded individuals, specialists, and new clients. Attend activities where you may meet others who share your interests and ambitions. Participate in these events by introducing yourself, participating in discussions, and following up with people you meet.

6. Add value and be generous: Networking is about more than just what you can get; it is also about what you can offer. Offer your talents and resources to assist others without expecting instant recompense. You establish oneself as a useful and trustworthy link by being giving. Those who have benefited them are more likely to be remembered and recommended.

7. _Maintain and nurture your network:_ Building a network is a continuous process that demands continual effort. Maintain contact with your contacts, give assistance, congratulate them on their achievements, and show real interest in their careers. Check in on a regular basis, provide useful articles or resources, and ask them to coffee or virtual meetings. Building and sustaining connections takes time and effort.

In summary, successful networking tactics and approaches are critical in today's linked society. You may unlock chances and improve your career or business by defining clear objectives, forming real relationships, being proactive, focusing on your communication skills, leveraging online platforms, attending industry-specific events, offering value, and maintaining your network. Remember that networking is a lifetime talent, and every connection you build has the potential to help you succeed.

7.3 COLLABORATING FOR SYNERGY AND MUTUAL SUCCESS

The ancient saying "two heads are better than one" could not be more applicable in today's fast-paced and competitive society. Collaboration has become an essential component for attaining success in many areas of life, including business, academia, and even personal relationships. The value of cooperation rests in its potential to generate synergy, in which individuals' combined efforts and views not only improve the quality of outputs but also stimulate mutual growth and success.

So, what are the keys to effective collaboration that can result in synergy and mutual success? Let us now look at some key principles:

1. Shared Vision and Goals: When all parties involved have a shared vision and goals, collaboration becomes genuinely successful. When people connect their goals and desires, the collective energy and focus propels them toward a single goal. By explicitly establishing and discussing these goals, everyone is on the same page and efforts can be directed toward cooperatively accomplishing them.

2. *Trust and Respect:* Trust is the cornerstone for effective cooperation. Without trust, open conversation, teamwork, and idea exchange become difficult. Building trust needs mutual respect, active listening, appreciating varied opinions, and upholding promises. When partners feel free to voice their perspectives and ideas without fear of being judged, it generates a trusting environment that supports invention and creativity.

3. *Effective Communication:* The foundation of every successful partnership is clear, open, and effective communication. This includes active listening, effectively communicating ideas, and offering constructive criticism. Collaborators should strive for clarity in order to ensure that everyone knows the roles and responsibilities. Transparent and consistent communication aids in the avoidance of misunderstandings, the resolution of problems, and the maintenance of a healthy working relationship.

4. ***Complementary Talents and Abilities:*** When individuals bring a broad range of talents, experience, and views to the table, collaborations thrive. Each collaborator brings distinct skills and talents to the table, which when combined result in a more comprehensive solution or conclusion. Recognizing and leveraging these diverse skills creates a synergistic effect that improves the collaboration's overall effectiveness and success.

5. *Adaptation and Flexibility:* Successful partnerships need adaptation and flexibility. New obstacles and possibilities may occur as the project or objective progresses. Being open to revising methods, changing plans, and accepting change helps collaborators to effectively negotiate these adjustments. When faced with hurdles, flexibility enables for creativity and creative problem-solving, allowing colleagues to adapt and develop new alternatives.

6. *Conflict Resolution:* When different viewpoints and ideas are brought together, conflicts are unavoidable. The key to successful teamwork, however, is how disputes are handled. Collaborators should approach problems with an open mind, finding resolutions that satisfy all parties while maintaining the collaboration's integrity.Conflicts may be transformed into opportunities for development and progress by emphasizing compromise, active listening, and a focus on finding win-win solutions.

7. Recognize and Learn from Setbacks:

Recognizing both large and little accomplishments is critical for generating motivation and keeping momentum within a collaborative project. Recognizing and praising individual and group achievements fosters a good and satisfying work environment. Setbacks and failures should also be regarded as learning experiences rather than obstacles. Collaborators may learn from losses and alter plans and approaches to achieve better success as a group.

Collaboration is an effective means of establishing synergy and mutual success. When people get together to share their knowledge and work toward a common goal, they unleash their collective potential. Collaborators create an environment conducive to achieving exceptional results by incorporating the secrets of successful collaboration, such as having a shared vision, building trust, effective communication, leveraging complementary skills, being flexible, resolving conflicts, and celebrating achievements. Together, they may overcome individual constraints and accomplish far more than they could individually, paving the way for joint success.

Chapter 8

MINDFULNESS AND WELLBEING: BALANCING SUCCESS AND HAPPINESS

The notion of success frequently dominates our thoughts and actions in today's fast-paced and highly competitive environment. We strive for success in our jobs, relationships, and personal accomplishments. However, the quest of achievement can often come at the expense of our pleasure and well-being. This is when mindfulness practice comes in handy.

The art of being completely present and aware of the current moment without judgment is known as mindfulness. It entails paying attention to our thoughts, feelings, and body sensations and embracing them without becoming caught up in a never-ending loop of self-criticism or judgment. We may reach a profound feeling of wellbeing and harmony by practicing mindfulness even while pursuing achievement.

Here are some mindfulness-based tips for balancing success and happiness:

1. Embrace the journey: Success is frequently viewed as a goal, but genuine satisfaction is found in embracing the journey. Mindfulness enables us to enjoy each moment rather than always looking forward to the next accomplishment. We may discover joy and fulfillment in the road toward our objectives if we are completely present and involved in what we are doing.

2. Let Go of Attachments: Our attachments to certain objectives can frequently lead to tension and disappointment. We may learn to let go of our expectations and accept whatever happens when we practice mindfulness. This does not imply abandoning our ambitions, but rather striking a balance between ambition and surrender to the current moment.

3. Make Self-Care a Priority: Success may be demanding and stressful, leaving little time for self-care. However, self-care is critical for general wellness and avoiding burnout. Mindfulness teaches us to prioritize our physical, emotional, and mental health by participating in activities that nourish and revitalize us. This might involve physical activity, meditation, spending time in nature, or engaging in activities that offer us delight.

4. Develop Gratitude: Gratitude is an extremely effective tool for happiness and joy. When we practice mindfulness, we become more conscious of our life' riches and cultivate a grateful attitude. By concentrating on what we are grateful for, we change our emphasis from what we lack to what we already have, generating a sense of fullness and happiness.

5. Strive for Work-Life Balance: Achieving a balance between work and personal life is critical for overall well-being. Mindfulness allows us to devote our complete attention to the present moment, allowing us to be totally present at work and with our loved ones. We may achieve balance in our work and personal lives by setting clear boundaries and emphasizing self-care.

Finally, mindfulness is a useful tool for balancing achievement and pleasure. It encourages us to slow down and enjoy the present moment, to let go of attachments, to prioritize self-care, to develop appreciation, and to achieve work-life balance. We may attain success without sacrificing our mental, emotional, and physical well-being by incorporating mindfulness into our lives, leading to a more satisfying and pleasant existence.

8.1 PRIORITIZING MENTAL AND PHYSICAL WELLBEING

Prioritizing one's mental and physical well-being is not only essential for living a good and satisfying life, but it is also one of the secrets to success. Taking care of our mental and physical health sometimes takes a second place in today's fast-paced environment, when the pressures of job, family, and personal commitments may be overwhelming. However, disregarding these important components of our life can have a negative impact on our general well-being and impede our performance in a variety of areas.

Here are some of the main reasons why prioritizing mental and physical well-being is a success secret:

1. Improved Focus and Productivity: When our mental and physical health are in balance, we can nurture maximum focus and productivity. Exercise on a regular basis Healthy dietary habits, enough sleep, and stress management skills all lead to enhanced mental clarity, energy levels, and less distractions. We may tackle activities and obstacles more efficiently with a clear and concentrated mind, helping us to do more in less time.

2. Increased Resilience: Life is full of ups and downs, as well as setbacks and failures. Individuals who emphasize their mental and physical well-being, on the other hand, are often better ready to face challenges with resilience. Engaging in mental health activities such as meditation, mindfulness, and relaxation techniques can help build emotional resilience and offer the inner power to recover from difficult experiences. Similarly, regular exercise strengthens the body and increases physical stamina, allowing people to endure challenging times

3. *Better Problem-Solving Skills:* Caring for our mental and physical health promotes cognitive functioning, including our capacity to think critically and solve issues. Regular physical activity boosts blood flow to the brain, encouraging neuroplasticity, which is necessary for memory learning and problem solving. Additionally, activities that promote mental well-being, such as reading, writing, or engaging in creative endeavors, can broaden our knowledge and drive inventive thinking.

4. *Improved Emotional Intelligence:* Mental and physical well-being are intertwined with emotional intelligence, which is critical to personal and professional success. Prioritizing self-care assists us to have a better awareness of our own and other people's emotions. We can manage stress, resolve disagreements, and communicate effectively when we are in touch with our feelings and have good coping skills, building healthier interpersonal connections.

5. Long-Term Sustainability: Success is more than simply meeting short-term objectives; it is also about ensuring long-term viability. Prioritizing mental and physical health ensures that we have the endurance, resilience, and general health to continue our performance. Neglecting these crucial factors can result in burnout, health problems, and diminished motivation, limiting our capacity to achieve our goals and attain our full potential.

Finally, including mental and physical well-being into our everyday lives is not a luxury but a must for success. We may improve our attention, productivity, resilience, problem-solving abilities, emotional intelligence, and long-term sustainability by addressing our mental and physical health. Adopting self-care activities such as exercise, good food, mindfulness, and stress management allows us to live more balanced and satisfying lives, allowing us to succeed in a variety of areas. So, remember that the key to success is to first and foremost take care of ourselves.

8.2 THE BENEFIT OF MINDFULNESS PRACTICES

Mindfulness techniques have grown in popularity in recent years, and for good cause. From stress management to general well-being, the benefits of adopting mindfulness into one's daily practice are numerous and may even contribute to success secrets. Here are a few examples of how mindfulness techniques may help and improve success in several aspects of life:

1. Improved Focus and Concentration: One of the most important aspects of success is the capacity to remain focused on the work at hand. Individuals who practice mindfulness learn to focus their attention on the present moment and develop a heightened feeling of awareness. Improved attention and concentration may lead to enhanced production efficiency and, as a result, better results in both personal and professional undertakings.

2. Reduced Stress and Increased Resilience:
Success frequently necessitates navigating difficult conditions and overcoming hurdles. Mindfulness activities are powerful strategies for stress management and resilience building. Individuals who have the capacity to notice thoughts and emotions without judgment can better respond to pressures and keep a calm and collected mentality, improving problem-solving abilities and flexibility.

3. Improved Emotional Intelligence: Emotional intelligence is critical to success. Mindfulness techniques encourage self-awareness and emotional control, helping people to better comprehend their own experiences and emotions. This self-awareness, together with the ability to empathize with others, improves interpersonal connections, effective communication, and leadership abilities.

4. Improved Decision-Making: Sound decision-making is critical for success in any sector. Mindfulness activities promote a state of conscious awareness, allowing people to make decisions with clarity and objectivity rather than impulsively or reactively. Mindfulness promotes superior judgment and decision-making abilities by pausing to ponder and consider alternative points of view.

5. Increased originality and Innovation: Success frequently necessitates originality and the capacity to think outside of the box. Mindfulness techniques promote a curious and open-minded perspective. Individuals can tap into their inner creativity to discover innovative solutions to problems or challenges by quieting the noise of the mind and establishing a receptive state.

It is critical to understand that mindfulness practices are neither a fast cure or a one-size-fits-all answer to attaining success. Rather, they are a helpful tool that may improve many elements of one's personal and professional life. Consistent practice and perseverance are required to cultivate mindfulness, but the long-term rewards are well worth the effort.

Incorporating mindfulness activities into one's daily routine may have a significant influence on one's general well-being and contribute to success secrets. Individuals may unleash their full potential and prosper in their undertakings by gaining greater attention, controlling stress, enhancing emotional intelligence, making better judgments, and boosting creativity. So, why not begin on a mindfulness journey and witness the transforming influence it can have on your success path?

8.3 INTEGRATING WELLBEING PRACTICES INTO YOUR DAILY ROUTINE

Integrating wellness routines into your everyday routine can considerably improve your overall life success. Taking care of your physical, mental, and emotional health is critical to reaching your objectives and having a happy life. Here are some tips for properly incorporating wellness habits into your everyday routine:

1. Make Self-Care a Priority: Make yourself a priority by scheduling self-care activities every day. Whether it's a bath, reading a book, practicing meditation, or engaging in a pastime, make time to refresh and revitalize.

2. *Mindfully Begin Your Day:* Begin your day with a thoughtful morning ritual. Rather of grabbing for your phone first thing in the morning, do something that promotes inner serenity and clarity. This might be sitting quietly and making objectives for the day ahead, or it could include meditation writing.

3. *Move Your Body:* Physical activity is essential for general health and well-being. Include exercise in your everyday routine, whether it's taking a stroll, going to the gym, practicing yoga, or dancing. Find activities that you like and incorporate them into your daily routine.

4. *Practice Gratitude:* Taking the time to recognize your benefits has a significant influence on your mental health. Develop a thankfulness habit by writing down a few things you're thankful for every day. This simple gesture can redirect your attention to the positive and enhance your entire view on life.

5. *Fuel Your Body with Nutritious Food:* A nutritious diet is essential to your general well-being. Make deliberate choices to nurture your body with nutritious meals. Consume fruits, vegetables, healthy grains, lean proteins, and lots of water. Avoid eating too many processed meals, sugary snacks, and beverages.

6. *Make Friends:* Human interactions are vital for our emotional well-being. Make an effort to maintain frequent contact with friends, family, and loved ones. Spend time with them, discuss your views and feelings, and encourage one another. Positive connections may boost your sense of satisfaction and contentment.

7. *Manage Stress:* Stress is an inevitable part of life, but good stress management is critical for general well-being. Use stress-reduction strategies such as deep breathing exercises, mindfulness meditation, or soothing hobbies such as listening to music or going on a nature walk. Find out what works best for you and implement it into your daily routine.

8. *Get Adequate Sleep:* Adequate sleep is a critical component of healthy health. Establish a consistent sleep routine and create a comfortable sleep environment to make sleep a priority. To prepare your mind and body for good sleep, avoid coffee and digital displays before bed and practice relaxation techniques.

Remember that incorporating wellness habits into your everyday routine is a long-term commitment. Developing good behaviors takes time, patience, and persistence. While navigating this road, be gentle to yourself and allow for flexibility. Prioritizing self-care in your daily routine will considerably help your overall success and well-being.

CONCLUSION

EMBRACING YOUR POTENTIAL FOR SUCCESS

Success is a very personal and subjective term that differs from person to person. However, there are some secrets and ideas that might help us achieve our goals and reach our full potential. We may unleash our latent skills, overcome challenges, and live a satisfying and meaningful life by adopting these success secrets.

Self-belief is one of the key secrets of success. It is critical that we have faith in our talents and potential. When faced with difficulties or failures, we are more prone to give up. We may tap into our inner power and persist despite hurdles by creating a positive mindset and having a can-do attitude.

Setting specific and attainable goals is also essential. Successful people have a clear picture of what they want to accomplish and divide their goals into doable tasks. This method aids in providing concentration, direction, and motivation. By defining specific goals and constantly monitoring progress we may stay on track and make steady progress towards our ambitions.

Another secret is the power of lifelong learning. Successful people are constantly upgrading their knowledge and talents. The world is continually changing, and in order to remain competitive, we must stay up to date on the newest innovations in our respective industries.

. This might include reading books, attending seminars, furthering one's education, or seeking advice from individuals who have previously achieved success. We may obtain the tools and knowledge we need to excel by consistently investing in our own growth and development.

Another important part of success is the development of resilience and flexibility. Life is full of unexpected hurdles and setbacks, and how we respond to these hardships can decide our level of success. Resilient people recover from failure, learn from their mistakes, and adjust their plans accordingly. They see setbacks as chances for growth and use them to strengthen their character and resilience. We may negotiate the ever-changing landscape of life with grace and resolve if we embrace change and are adaptable in our approach.

Finally, success is a collective journey rather than a solitary attempt. Surrounding oneself with a supporting network of like-minded people is a secret that many successful people share. We may gain direction, motivation, and inspiration by surrounding ourselves with good influencers, mentors, and helpful peers. Collaboration may boost our potential and open doors to opportunities we would not have explored otherwise.

Finally, believing in your own potential for success necessitates self-belief, explicit goal setting, ongoing learning, resilience, flexibility, and a supporting network. Success is a lifetime goal, not an overnight thing. It takes commitment, hard effort, and perseverance. We may unleash our entire potential, achieve our objectives, and live a life of fulfillment, purpose, and brilliance by implementing these success secrets. So embrace your potential, believe in yourself, and take the necessary actions to make your aspirations a reality. The path may be difficult, but the rewards are priceless.